Words
of
Friction

A collection of poetry & prose

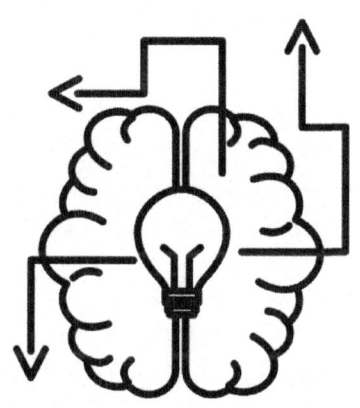

By D.B. Wright

Copyright © 2021 D.B.Wright

All rights reserved. No Part of this publication may be reproduced, distributed, or transmitted in any form or by any means, including photocopying, recording, or other electronic or mechanical methods, without the prior written permission of the publisher, except in the case of brief quotations embodied in critical reviews and certain other non-commercial uses permitted by copyright law.

Paperback ISBN: 978-1-9168779-0-0

DEDICATION

This book is dedicated to everyone who believed in me, and everyone who doubted me. In equal measures you have fueled my hopes and dreams.

And, of course, to my wife and baby boy who are my everything.

FORWARD FROM THE AUTHOR

My love affair with words began as early as I can remember. I always read, or was read to, as a child. I would read, learn, recite and reimagine all the stories in all the books in our house. It was my escape and my joy.

Then, like with many love affairs, we drifted apart. I was seduced by other distractions – sports, computer games, films, girls. I would occasionally turn my attention back to words, and for periods of time the flame would rage again, only to fade away to the next fad or distraction.

This pattern continued for way too many years. Years full of love, happiness, sadness, pleasures, pains, ups and downs, mistakes, regrets, rises and falls, right turns and wrong turns, and all the things a life brings. Through all that time I was lacking that one ingredient I subconsciously knew I craved.

Then, one day my subconscious and consciousness met. I imagine them bumping into each other at a book shop holding the same novel, and both awkwardly apologising before catching gazes and a falling for each other.

To use a shorter metaphor, the penny finally dropped. I needed words in my life, and not just other peoples. I needed to write. What followed was a tsunami of ideas which had been swirling in my mind for all those years. Word after word, Page after page, of writing. Some of those words found their way into stories, others into blog posts, and many others into poetry.

It's the poems which I am delighted to present to you in this book. I have titled this collection "Works of Friction".

.

I have divided this collection in to broad categories: Pain, Love, thoughts & reflections. In truth, many of the poems traverse multiple categories, or don't bare categorizing at all. These poems are the aggregate result of my poetry journey so far, and each one is presented to you with a humble and grateful heart.

Thank you for reading.
D.B.Wright

CONTENTS

Acknowledgments i

1 On Pain 7

2 On Love 63

3 Thoughts and Reflections 108

ACKNOWLEDGMENTS

I am eternally grateful to Mira Hadlow, my hugely talented friend who was the first person to make me believe in my words. Her kindness and encouragement seem limitless; believe me, I have tested those limits.

To all the other writers, readers, online followers, and friends I've met along the way: I appreciate and respect you all.

To my mom: I realise now that the spark came from you.

ON PAIN

I have seen my fair share of pain, trauma and loss in my life; my own and that of others. I have fought battles with demons, and assisted others fight similar battles. I have also borne witness to inspirational moments of healing, recovery, and displays of human resilience and resolve beyond measure.

As a writer, I feel a sense of duty to write about all topics, no matter how difficult or challenging it may be. I believe that expressing our thoughts is a vital step towards growing our understanding and acceptance of ourselves and each other.

The following are a collection of writings which cover pain, suffering, loss and trauma. The reader should note that the poems in this section of the book touch on difficult topics and may contain emotive descriptions and imagery.

"Is there no way out of my mind?"
-Sylvia Plath

Sometimes

Sometimes, when I'm lost,
or found in thought,
I think of you.
I say sometimes;
all the time.

First, during the worst,
it was ice cold
to think of your face,
and your smile I'd trace
with lost fingers.

Last, in warm grass,
like sunshine
across my mind.
You being mine;
most times.

Today, through thick grey,
I recede to you,
remember you,
cherish you.

Sometimes. All the time.

White Gold

"Mom. I don't want you to die."
"I've got to die one day.."
"Yeah....but please....not today."

Then she slipped away...
Quietly...
Peacefully...
She was 83.

Genetically,
she was fifty percent of me,
but, in reality,
she was the best of me.
To my zany soul,
she was pure White Gold.
Her stories and jokes
never got old,
and will stay told.

She Writes

She writes
Like her soul set fire
to her heart
And her pen
Is extinguishing
The flames.

She sings
Like betrayal left
Her blood frozen
And her voice
Is thawing
Her veins.

She plays guitar
Like the strings
Are her disgraces
And her nails
Scratch away
the shame.

She dances
Like plague rats
Blight her psyche
And her feet
Stamp away
The pain.

She lashes out
Like crazed hornets
Haunt her spirit
And her hands
Are weapons
Of rage.

She cries
Like life left
Her broken
And her tears
Are warm
Healing rain.

She prays
Like her wings
Were stolen
And her pleas
Will grant her
Flight again.

God Stained

She was god stained and hell made;
Her sparkle bore a weight of shame.

She was storm drenched and sun dried;
Raging rivers and calming tides.

She knew feral and she knew swoon;
Laughed and cried beneath full moons.

She had angel eyes with demonic hues;
Angry scars under winged tattoos.

She yearned to be touched in isolation
But flinched at thoughts of adoration.

She danced to music no one cared for
And sobbed to films about trust.

She spoke fondly of the devil's tooth
But lilies adorned her prayer-books.

She floated around her own loneliness;
A tranced moth to her own flame.

She screamed her anger at the oceans
But whispered sorrow to the breeze.

She wore shoes to match expectations
And a smile to cover hobbled pain.

She walked like nothing ever mattered
And crawled when something did.

Scar Cycle

It was a cycle of pain and baiting;
He'd kiss the scars he created.

It was a carousel of hurt and persuasion;
Angry nights and soppy mornings.

It was fragile porcelain adoration;
He'd glue the pieces he'd broken.

It was a furnace of burning emotions;
He'd snuff out fires he ignited.

It was a game of gaslit confrontation;
He'd begin and end all conversation.

It was a storm of forgive and anticipation;
Fresh starts and final chances.

It was a vortex of regret and instigation;
Soft sorrow for hard aggression.

It was a helter-skelter of damnation;
Cracked bones and shattered synapses.

It was time to enact her retribution;
A savage and brutal retaliation.

It was an ending of winged elation;
She freed the soul he'd incarcerated.

He'd cry

He'd cry;
He'd hit me,
Then he'd cry.
Sometimes during,
but usually after,
The beat and the batter.
He'd Thump and kick me,
Until his lungs lacked capacity,
Then, with ghoulish audacity,
He'd cry.

He'd cry;
Him...not me!
Like a chastised child
Or an un-fed baby.
At first I thought maybe
It was pent up sadness,
Or a moment madness,
He seemed so tragic
Weak and pathetic,
He'd cry.

He'd cry;
Staring at me
With owlish eyes.
Begging and pleading.
Weak wimpish tears,
Accompanied by whines.
High pitched pines;
His...NOT mine!
Grating my weary mind.
He'd cry.

He'd cry;
Episodically,
Get fired and riled.
I'd say what I could

To soften his wild,
Incessant rage.
Urge the anger to fade.
"I'm sorry I made you do this babe!"
He'd cry.

He'd cry;
Sad-angrily
He'd let fly.
By the time I asked
"What's the matter?"
His body would shake,
His teeth chatter.
And I'd feel the clatter,
or worse a shatter.
Agonising disaster.
He'd cry.

He'd cry;
It was sweet to me
I don't know why.
I was lost, perhaps,
In the aftermath.
Lungs gasping,
Hearts thumping,
Sweat pouring,
And tears falling
Down our faces,
Stinging at grazes,
Mocking our disgraces,
He'd cry

He'd cry;
Penetrate me
And whine.
Often, I'd vomit
From the pain,
And a punch-drunk brain.
But mostly from the shame
Of being here again,

About to take the blame,
Wondering which one of us
Was actually insane.
He'd cry.

He'd cry;
Rape me,
Then he'd try,
To desperately deny;
Tell the same lies,
The ones I despised,
But I welcomed reprise,
From the strain.
So, taking the blame
Wasn't really that insane?
He'd cry.

He'd cry;
After breaking me.
And I'd decree,
If just perhaps,
This time would be the last,
We could put it in the past.
That there'd be no relapse.
I must have been tapped;
The cycle had me trapped!
He'd cry.

He'd cry;
He'd hit me
Then he'd cry.
Sob and bawl,
Like a fool.
So, I stabbed him.
Slammed his head off a wall.
It worked;
He twitched and jerked,
Squealed and lurched.
The tables were turned.
Roles reversed.

Torture reimbursed,
As so often rehearsed.
I felt cold and perverse.
But hell knows it was deserved.

And I cried.

Lycanthropy

She gripped the rim of the porcelain sink and tried to steady her hands. "One last time", she whispered to herself. One. Last. Time.

Yellow teeth;
Blood stained and itching,
Lengthen from her gums,
Wobbling on searching tongue.
Metallic tastes mix with blood.

Long Lycanthropic fingers
Gape open her mouth,
Dip down to grizzly tonsils,
Scratching vomitous chords
For a final encore.

One. Last. Time.
Never again after this.

No more turning savage
At moon shaped plates.
No more feast and famine.
No more hurling in shadows.

She's never going to turn again.

Tomorrow she rises
With the sun
To healing brunch.
Waffles and bacon,
Coffee and juice.

And she will let herself replete.
Tomorrow.

For now, she'll release
One. Last. Time.
Wild and free.

Negotiable Affection

Misty moves
But not for them;
Not for these.. "men";
Thinking themselves wolves
Presenting as starved pigs.

Hips swing and sway
With absent minded intent,
Curving out her rent,
Gliding skin and bones
To ballad rock-and-roll.

She moves to the tunes
But not to their beats.
She dances half-hinged;
Just enough looseness in the hips,
The perfect measure of want in the lips,
Slowly coaxing the biggest tips.
Pushing and pulling, just the right teases.
Tempering excitement, encouraging keenness

Oh, She knows which ones
Have bigger egos than pockets
And which have more pocket than sense,
Marking the latter for special attention.

She'll go further
With the right persuasion;
The correct cash injection.
A fairly negotiated affection
Funding her happy-ever-after
With their happy endings.
Hot earned cash
Pressed against lustless goosebumps.

All of it is for them -
Her beautiful boys.

She spends this time
Handing out delights
To these creatures of the night
So her boys can survive, or thrive,
Knowing there's always that chance they'll
end up just like these.. "men".

Better than never having had a choice at all.

Numb

I don't feel, anymore
I just think thoughts.
I don't try, anymore
I press play and record.

I'm not a freak, anymore
I'm differently normal.
I'm not hurt, anymore
They are not able.

I won't hide, anymore
Caught in a bubble.
I'm not lost, anymore
I'm perfectly troubled.

I don't dream, anymore
It keeps me awake.
I don't need, anymore
Nothing left to take.

I'm not myself, anymore
They are more like me.
I'm not trying, anymore
You are not like me.

I can't lay here, anymore
This is their bed.
I won't speak, anymore
Everything is said.

I'm not here, anymore
I'm outside inside.
I'm not going, anymore
It's too far to find.

I won't cry, anymore
They gave me the drugs.
I'm not down, anymore
They are wrongly up.

I won't laugh, anymore
They take all the funny.
I don't stand, anymore
Freedom is fallacy.

I won't fight, anymore
They took away my fists.
I won't flight, anymore
I'm stable and hooked.

I'm not young, anymore
They keep on reminding.
I'm not cool, anymore
I'm stuck undecided.

It's not me, anymore
Versions of Immersion.
It's not them, anymore
Versions of divergence.

I can't see you, anymore
They told me your name.
I won't listen, anymore
I'm numb to the pain.

I can't shine, anymore
They made me like rain.
I won't rise, anymore
I'm numb to the pain.

I won't live, anymore
They tell me I'm saved.
I won't lie, anymore
I'm numb to the pain.

Unbearable

My ears can't bare the weight of the words the sorrowful mid-wife says.
They could bleed rivers, to muffle the noise and wash out audio pain.
The sound of throbbing blood is preferable to this dreadful tale.
The brain, incredulous, denies all knowledge and departs itself away;
Expunging the moment from near memory,
Passing responsibility to vascular array.
But, my heart gives up all it's known rhythms; instead thumping out random quakes.
Blood rushes in all directions, overwhelmed by this new reality, it seeks to find escape.
My lungs, react with contraction removing all but a few grams of Breath.
My throat closes, as if sealing further agony from my delicate internal depths.
My tongue dances to a nonsensical language, spinning itself in knotted sadness.
My bladder, winces, squeezes and pinches,
Sending warm ounces dripping down trembling thighs.
Mournful knees buckle beneath me in desperation and despair.
My stomach explodes a purge bomb to flood the poisonous knowledge out,
Deep drawn bitter bile burns my esophagus, and stings my throat and mouth.
I beg for my eyes to be plucked from their sockets, and jammed Inside my ears,
So I do not have to see or hear this miserable moment for a single second more.

Evergreen

She's felt lashes of pain few could understand.
Held pieces of teeth and flesh in broken hands.
Borne the weight of her elders sins
All the way back to her beginnings.
Her ears have craved silence between
Her own excruciating screams.
Blades have painted pictures across her Peleus skin.
Body ravaged, soul savaged,
Bent bones have begged for relief.

Despite all this, she's evergreen.

Her mouth whispers in imaginary muses;
Some abusers, some want to be abused.
Her throat has been battered and bruised,
Choked by raging hands and rotten foods.
Her lips have stuck to forced disgorges;
Throat disfigured, voice distorted.
There's stink and stains on all her organs.
Spine has bowed through demonic contortions;
Creeks creep through cracked cartilages.

Despite all this, she's evergreen.

Her feet have left bloody prints on moonlit sand and grass
Scar-patterned like tire tracks,
Ridged and ribboned by shattered beer glass.
Her legs buckled by bone cracks.
    Satanic attacks.
 On racks.
       Arched back.
            Clawed and scratched.

But, still she dances with grace and glee,
Spinning barefoot, unafraid and free.
She's evergreen.

Her scarred tongue has tasted metallic agony.
Felt sharp prongs and white heat.
Inhaled her own burning meat.
Been slowly stung by rampant disease.
Succumb to the most depraved deeds.
On back, all fours or on her Knees.
Swallowed up unwanted seeds.
She owns no broken dreams;
For, dreams have never been.
All she's known are horror scenes.
How to stay alive, survive and bleed.
From porcelain babe to fractured teen.

Despite all this, she's evergreen.

She's stood in the ashes of the house of devils,
Having burned down their reign of evil.
Grinning at the flickering flames,
Cackling and howling their wicked names.
Ignoring their desperate mercy pleas.
A caged bird on the edge of freedom.
A Phoenix embracing its emancipation.
A lost soul found in fiery consecration.
She has escaped the satanic womb;
Been re-birthed fresh and new.

Tortured princess,
Reborn a queen.
Savage and free,
She's evergreen.

Slipstream

I remember what it was like to be normal
So I do an impression of that,
And hope that nobody notices
It's all a delicate act.

I used to relish socialising,
With eclectic, hectic friends.
Now, I just go through motions
Hoping they don't note the pretence.

I partition my existence
in to false shiny pieces.
Sweet treats and objects
I do not want or need.

I congregate my virtues
On a phoney social feed,
To substitute inaction
With egotistical relief.

I day dream of a childish past
Where, In quiet anarchy,
Warm Innocence casts
A long shadow back to me.

I call upon my better self;
Compliant, successful, sane,
And I hang on to his coattails
Being dragged from day to day.

Occasionally, in the quiet hours,
There are times I feel almost alive,
Lost with precious thoughts and words,
Set free by rhythm and rhyme.

But most the time I'm outside myself;
An observer of a dour dream.
Distant and different to everyone else,
Existing in the slipstream.

Alcohol Kisses

I don't remember summer days that rained.
It's funny that, how a brain
Protects and deflects from itself,
Keeps all the colour, and edits out the grey.
Or hides the rain.

There's a lot of things I don't remember.
Until I do.
They creep into consciousness with silent steps.
They peep into innocent moments dressed as fear and regret.
Tap me on the shoulder, shivering my cortex.

I don't recall their breath on the back of my neck, until a certain light
breeze catches me off guard and steals my calmness.
Then my mind unwinds and regresses back to distressing indiscretions.

I don't recall the stench of alcohol and vomit creeping in to the room
ahead of them, like a bilious scouting party.
Odours joined by cigarettes and over-sprayed hair as they drew closer,
Then the additional stink of their feet as they kicked off their shoes.

My minds ear can't quite hear the word "SHUSH" hisspered through
petrified darkness.
Woken from bad dreams into worse nightmares.
Out of the frying pan into the fire.
Out of innocence into their desires.

"That's not a proper kiss!"
I used to kiss them on the lips.
No! THEY used to kiss ME on the lips.
Touch my most personal bits;
The parts my parents said were "private",
But, "that rule doesn't count for aunties".
That's how it ended and started,
With those lies and deceits.

I don't recall the taste of my tears on their hands as they covered my pleading mouth, until a sad song or random documentary traces tears down my face,
and the taste
reminds me why I don't cry.

I can't remember their muffled sighs as they finally found their relief.
On the good nights they'd leave,
But usually they'd fall to sleep
Snoring and farting on top me.

I don't recall being drenched in urine -
mine, theirs or both - until a vividly remembered nightmare brings it all literally flooding back to my sheets.
"He's wet the bed again! Dirty little bastard!"

I don't remember December sunshine.
Funny that, how a brain
Forsakes and betrays
Edits out the colour, keeps only grey shades.

They never had to deny it
Because I never uttered a word.
Until I did.

Albert Street

Kelly's off at quarter past six,
After a 13 hour blissful shift
With sporadic abuse,
Blood, piss and shit.

She'd love to head straight home,
hold her boys and Snuggle.
Promise them an end to strife,
And take away the struggle.

But Kelly's got a thing to hide,
A stop to make with swallowed pride.
She won't have her kids denied
And this time she won't cry.

(I won't cry)

Albert street community centre
Where, in the 80s, she'd hang out,
And around,
And about,
With the usual suspects.
A collection of rejects;
Young, unwise and wet.
Four cans get wrecked.
Usually wretch,
Speaking of which,
Her first snog with 'clitch'
Almost shagged him;
But didn't.
Not that time.

(Not that time!)

One pound fifty for entry,
Crisps, drink, use of facilities.
Open to all colours and creeds.

Special, or un-special needs.
Different, or indifferent abilities.
All strengths and agilities.
An eclectic and hectic
Elevation from poverty.
Release from the misery.

(I wish I had one pound fucking fifty now.)

Albert street was shut by '94
Couldn't find the funds no more.
Locals were outraged,
But failed to engage.
A few complained,
Kicked off a campaign.
She remembered walking in rain.
Road to road,
Door to Door,
As down it poured.
Some donated
What they could afford.
Some swore and roared.
While others were just bored.

(Probably dead most of those people now)

Then the forgotten years.
The building left to rotting years.
Disused and disowned,
But remained a renowned
secret meet up point
For clandestine illegality;
Elicit, sometimes solicit,
hook ups.
Used by dossers, druggies
And fuck-ups,
For consumption of one thing,
Or consummation of another.
Often both.

(I was young and stupid!)

Now, here she was in 2020 at
Albert Street dispensary.
Handouts-a-plenty!
A food redistribution hive
Of people with big hearts
And keen-kind minds,
Who carefully contrived
To assist the deprived,
Help them survive,
keep them alive.
Or at least living.
Desperate unfortunates
Who happen to bad times.
Who don't quite earn enough
From their graft and grind.
Or don't graft and grind at all,
Of them- there's some, for sure.
But she's not one of them.

(At least I'm not one of them. At least I fucking work)

Like in the 80s she's a regular now,
But never sure why or how.
She's ticking all of the right boxes;
Working hard, playing soft,
Resisting temptation,
Fending off annihilation,
Envisioning a destination,
Where her boys, in quiet restoration,
Rise up,
Wise up,
And discover a life
that's more than enough.
Or just enough will do-
Just a chance to breathe.

(It's never enough. I've had enough! I can't breathe)

The volunteers are lovely,
Chatty and bubbly.
But that doesn't make it better;
It makes it worse.
She'd rather they were terse,
Instead of this happy,
Unintentionally rehearsed,
Chapter and verse.
"Oh, you're a nurse?"

(YES I am a fucking nurse. And 20 minutes ago I was inserting a cannula in to an elderly gents arm. Now I'm stood here exchanging pleasantries in the most unpleasant place I can think of. Can we get on with it?)

Questions:
"Have you been here before?"
(Yes)
"How many are we shopping for?"
(Four)
But it's not shopping,
Not really!
She's not paying,
Not with money!
The price is pain,
And some self-distain.
A fair exchange;
Goods for Shame.
But.. Existence sustained;
Her boys eat again.
She loves her boys so much.

(I love my boys so much. I'm a good mother)

Just how much can a mother give?
How much?
This much?
Enough to be here?
"There's soup here my dear!"
Enough to do this?
"How about some crisps?"

"Oh look, PG Tips-
-how lucky"

(Lucky yeah..)

At least this time she didn't cry.

(I didn't cry!)

Black Noise

I would love to sleep without screaming and wake with calm dry eyes.
My nightmares give me daymares give me nightmares on repeat.
I want to be left alone with my precious thoughts without them shattering to pieces.
I have pleaded and pledged my soul to every known deity to grant me release.
These white and black noises torment and disturb me on cruel rotation,
Stinging my reality and suppressing my vivid imagination.
Until I'm left with nothing but stillness and an empty shell of discarded memories.

Strings begin to strum deep inside me, echoing lost tunes of nothingness.
Songs of ancient non-existence reverberating pithless sounds,
Between the lines of universal dissonance and nanoscopic ambience.
All there is and all there isn't at once.

At least this black noise is not the greyness which haunts my normality.
Where the white and black discordant orchestra crash and burn in my mind.
At least here I do not need to conduct, or be conducted by, the din.
At least here the light and shadows do not conspire to blind or bind me.
This onyx ocean of still breath and museless silence soothes turmoil and tumult.
Here, I am unshattered and unresolved; unnoticed and untouched.

Here, I am unborn.
Here, I am unawakened.
Here, I am unfree.

Little Penguin

Inhale.
Exhale.
Today, like all the hardest days,
I can't remember how to breathe.
I'm never sure if I've forgotten how
Or, if my sub-conscience somehow,
In deep-rooted rotting sorrow,
Does not want to allow
The simple in-and-out
Of chest bellows.

Inhale.
Exhale.
In, feels like swallowing hell.
Out, feels like pleading to heaven.
Each emission an invocation,
A bitter bilious exorcism,
Recited from my soul,
Interminable notes echoed
From mouth to twitching toes.
The desperate feeling grows
As further inhalations cool my mouth and nose,
Torturing my lungs and throat.

Inhale.
Exhale.
Each breath comes as a compromise
Between the instinct to survive
And a desire to just.. die.
For my soul to rise, softly glide,
Through polychromatic rays of light
And gleefully arrive, bright and fine,
To you; again mine.
And my heart,
On these days I wish it would stop beating.
Instead, it flaps loud and deafening;
Chaotic, Arrhythmic guilt

Pumping blood with discordant lilt.
I want to rip it from the chest hilt,
Watch it wither and wilt.

Inhale.
Exhale.
Simple lung expansion and contraction.
Opposite but symbiotic actions
That bless my blood but curse my soul.
Time is supposed to heal all wounds,
Slowly shine light in to darkened rooms,
Birth us from the excruciating wombs,
Unlock these chains of decaying gloom.
But time being a healer is a total ruse
Working only on physical cuts and bruises,
Failing to fix internal pain and abuses,
It doesn't get better it gets differently worse.
You never fully heal, just get used to the curse.

Inhale.
Exhale.
The moments between in and out are the most unbearable.
The frozen gap before painful inhalation turns to exhausted exhalation.
The pause between emptying lungs and unwanted repletion.
The silence between the ticks of a clock.
Deep chasmic quietness filled with dread and despair,
Where your face flashes my minds eye,
Like a printing press constantly hammering your visage to my psyche.
You're wearing the outfit bought to match your sweet nickname.
I was your polar bear and you were my little penguin.
You'd flap your tiny arms every time I picked you up.
I was planning to tell you when you were old enough that Polar Bears
and Penguins don't come from the same place.
But that was a long way off; you were still so teeny and new.

Inhale.
Exhale.
How many more times should I bother to breathe?
Ten times - for each precious toe;
Ten more times - for each delicate finger;

Fifty times - for each long eyelash framing Irish blue eyes;
A hundred more - for the fair hairs on the brows;
A thousand times - for each hair on your soft head;
Or,
Two times - for all the things that came in pairs;
Two ears with luscious little lobes.
Two nostrils with genetic flare.
Two eyes blue like mine.
Two chubby legs, I could just munch.
Two feet with curling toes.
Two little gloves on two little hands.
Two arms always flapping.
Two minutes until the blue lights.
Two hours until the doctors gave up.
Two grannies with broken hearts.
Two grandads waiting in the sky.

And two little dimples
In two little cheeks.
One for each month you were ours.

Inhale.
Exhale.
The idea of creating a new ending,
One in which I cease breathing,
Is always appealing,
always calling,
You're always calling,
I'm always falling..
The thought keeps bleating,
And the desire is unrelenting,
To hold you, my little penguin,
One more time.

An angel still has wings
Even if they cannot fly.

Shooting stars

The old rocking chair squeaked,
Like a chorus of agitated mice.
The pain in his knee
echoed their complaints
as he swayed back and forth.

In the early days It had never squeaked;
He wasn't sure when that had started.
It drove his wife mad but he kinda liked it
Now, he wouldn't fix that squeak
For all the money on the planet.

The room was trapped in forever,
Like every yesterday he could remember.
Left almost untouched,
Gathering unfriendly dust,
Which dulcified the atmosphere.

On the walls were stickers he'd carefully placed.
Even the rainbow he'd slightly ripped,
And delicately but unconvincingly fixed,
Hoping she'd not notice.
Which, of course, she did
But didn't cause a fuss about it.

Below the rainbow were tiny paint prints,
Ages ranging from zero up.
A stamped record of growth.
He recalled, with a smile, what a fuss
It had been to clean the paint
From little palms and feet.

On the wall opposite was the moon
And the forest animals looking up;
The rabbit, the bear and the fox.
His boy, like them, had dreamt of
Reaching the woman in the moon.

The curtains were fully closed
And that light was on;
The one that made the ceiling look like the cosmos.
Designed to invoke wonder and mystery.
With its bright spinning stars and galaxies.

The alcohol was starting to work it's uncharm
And his mind was losing its calm.
He draped his head back.
With fresh-wet owlish eyes
And a hot, woozy brain
He watched the cosmos dance,
Bobbing and gliding his body
In time with its familiar motions.

Eventually, his eyes settled left
To the empty cot;
The one he'd constructed himself.
His masculine contribution
To an otherwise wifeyfied room.
The vertical slats seemed like prison bars
But no child was incarcerated inside,
Only dust and Benjy Bunny,
Who he'd always found so cuddly.

Intoxication took further grip
And he began, again,
The dismal annual writ.
Starting with his shoes,
Which he slowly removed,
Left then right.
"Left, right"
He remembered them marching in the yard
With exaggerated legs and arms.
Fake soldiers but real bonds.

Trousers next, as per the ceremony.
Uncarefully and awkwardly,
Hip-shrugs and shimmies,

Kicking them off eventually.
His mind drifted inevitably
To the times he battled
With wild kicking legs
Angry at nappy changes.

His t-shirt was the same one
He'd been wearing
The last time he held him.
He eased it off over his head,
Deep-Sniffing as it passed over his face
Basking in how it retained a trace,
Of his little boy.

He arose from the chair,
Absent of any grace or flare,
Causing the squeaky blare
To lose its rhythm,
Momentarily becoming an orchestra
Of terrified vermin.
He pushed his underpants down
and lightly kicked them aside.
Leaving him fully naked and alone.

With lost limbs he traced
An unrhythmic dance
With the stars and planets
Then, with all the usual inelegance
He lofted himself in to the wooden prison
And slumped in fetal-position,
His thumb inside his mouth,
And benjy gripped between heart and breath.

The stars and galaxies above
Continued to spin and play,
As tears rolled from his eyes,
Like Shooting stars joining the cosmic ballet.

The Gap

Tonight, I'm dwelling on a tiny lost angel: Wondering if you feel the same amount of miss in your heavenly heart as I do in this mortal pit.

I'm wishing away the gaping chasm between here without you and there by your side. I'm wondering if you stare into the same chasm and make the same wish.

Sinister voices are suggesting how to close the gap: how a precisely placed snick on the correct artery could transport me to you.
Better voices remind me of the beauty I'd be leaving behind: the pain I'd leave behind.

I'm thinking about how guilty every second of my existence feels. Each breath of mortal air feels like I stole it from you. I wish I could barter my breaths for yours: trade places and allow you the precious life you deserved.

You have a brother now. He's nothing like you yet exactly the same. He's just about perfect. And so were you.

ID

She stepped in to a cold pale room,
Listless, grey and full of gloom.
Ghostly air provoked her skin
As an officer escorted her in.

Never before had her soul felt so alone
Like a lost child with no hands to hold,
But she was raised up brave and bold,
And this moment she owed herself to own.

She thought she knew what to expect;
Most think they do until they're met
With the coldest of cold realities.
It's impossible to ever be ready.

There exists no preparation,
No vivid type of imagination,
That can contrive the torturous agony
Of identifying your child's lifeless body.

The police had suggested
(And she had protested)
To do this via photographs,
Rather than in cold flesh.
An offer in a thousand lifetimes,
She could never accept.
That would have been neglect
Of mother-sister-daughterly duty.

As she stepped forward,
Her courage undressed.
Stripped itself from her mind
Exposing dread and distress.
Shaking, breaking breath.
A non-believer in an empty church.
Approaching its dire altar.

The body-bag conceals;
Inch by inch,
Slowly unzips to reveal.
Inch by inch,
Familiar features unveiled.
Inch by inch,
An interminable ordeal.
Inch by inch,
It doesn't seem real;
Until it is.

The bag pulls away,
And there she lay,
Her angel.
Hopelessly motionless.
Skin lotion-less;
Pale and porcelain,
Icy to touch,
But still you caress,
Trace and press
Her lifeless face
With lost fingers,
Letting your tips linger
On fading features,
Still clinging to radiance
Like a freshly picked flower.
Her hair, black as witch's ink.
Smooth and shiny
But deathly still;
Not waving or raving
Or "misbehaving"
In the ways that it had
Just yesterday morning.
Her smell like yellowed lavender fields
Shining in your chest
Growing daisies
With each breath.
And her eyes;
Dark, astray and distant.
Just a glimmer of her distinction;

A hint of her light,
Frozen in last night.

Confusion intrudes..

..denial the reaction;
As it is so often.
Self preservation;
A conspiratorial distraction
From the strangling realisation,
From the morbid vision,
Before you.

Can anything save you..

..The prayers follow;
Begging and pleading
To man, gods and idols.
Promise to be their disciple
If they are just able
To return your baby,
Untake your angel.
You beseech to her,
Willing her to hear your pain,
And miraculously return to you.
To be bound by bones
Swap her flesh and soul
With your own.
Bound by bones.

Maybe it's a mistake..

..Further denial;
Desperate and inventive,
Elaborate wild imaginings.
Irrational and relentless
Stories to allude and prove
She's still here with you.
Safe, soft and well.
This isn't your child lying here;

Its someone who looks like her!
"Who is this girl? Her poor mother."
"Its not her - Ellie's still alive!"
She survived,
And will thrive,
Live high and wise.
"Ellie is alive!"

Knees and tears fall to the floor..

..realisation,
An end to the imaginations
With no healing compensation.
Just sickening devastation.
Heart and breath begin pacing,
Stomach and mind churning
Mouth involuntarily salivating
In preparation of bilious vomiting.
Eyes doused out and dimmed.
Resilience trimmed.
"Ellie's dead".

Eyes and mind spring to wild life..

..Now manic-panic,
Partnered with anger.
Lashing out,
And around and about.
Violent convulsions.
Reversion to childhood temper tantrums;
Stamping and stomping and squealing
The soreness away.
Someone will pay.
Blasting and cursing the deities,
Whom, just now,
You'd afforded praises.
Framing and blaming,
Angrily castigating,
Everyone, and everything.
And yourself.

The blood in your veins mocks and stings your existence..

..Back to realisation.
Now partnered with resolve.
Wiping your tears,
Disguising your fears,
A strange calm and stillness
Dejected feebleness
Acceptance of circumstance.
Stoic and determined.
"Ellie's dead"

Flashes of Memories.

She recalls the room
Ellie was birthed.
Listless and clinical,
Like an empty church
Much like this one.
Room to room.
Womb to tomb.
Life to death.
"Ellie's dead".

An outpouring of every stage of grief compacted in to no more than half an hour; and all of it merely the opening act to a long, cruel, grieving play.

Lost

The night before last night
I lived a dark cold dream.
I'm standing on a lake of ice
In just shorts and an old tee.

I'm lost, or unfound,
Frigid and freezing.
There's mist all around
And my wrists are bleeding.

...I feel the blood flow...

The scene is framed
By evergreen trees,
Swinging and swaying
In chilly breezes.

In a starless sky
An over-sized moon
With a cartoon smile
Beams and swoons.

Unearthly sized birds
Float, Swoop and glide,
Whistling avian words
Flirting with moonlight.

Somewhere distant
A bell is ringing,
And there's a hint
Of something banging.

...ringing and banging...

I'm otherwise lost,
So I cling to those sounds,
Believing, If they stop,

I'll freeze or drown.

I try to take a step
But stumble slip and slide,
As my bare feet protest,
I fall down on the ice.

My hands search for grip.
Lungs gasp for relief.
The blood in my wrists
Continues to seep.

...I'm drifting away...

As suddenly as a sneeze
The moon turns crimson.
It's smile to a frown
A Luna Demon.

The birds circling the sky
Turn livid and heathen.
They spiral and gyre
Squawking and screaming.

The wintery breezes
Triple their strength
And the evergreen trees
Rock, Rattle and bend.

The distant bells
Seem lost in the hum.
The ground starts to throb
Like a beating war-drum.

I scramble to my feet but then..

Across the ice,
From all sides,
Dark figures rise,
With red eyes,

Flaming bright.
Horns white;
Bony spikes.
Covered in blight.
Black liquid seeps
From their skin
Like witches ink.
They start to slink,
Jolt and limp,
Over the rink.
Unsteadily,
And slowly,
Fixated to me.
A chorus
Of rusty
Pained groans,
And aching moans,
Accompany them
As they go.

...I'm statuesque in fear...

Pale ice beneath my feet
Begins to crack and fissure,
Hastening their reach,
Quickening my fear.

I look left and right,
Forward and back,
But the same demons rise,
And I am trapped.

I can just about make out
The ringing of the bell;
I feel there's no doubt
It's my guide from this hell.

So I run towards it...

But dream-drenched limbs,
The slippery lake,
And lack of shoes,
Hinder my escape.

Inevitably, I fall again,
And land on all-fours.
I slide the ice and spin.
And then I try to crawl.

The touch of bitter ice on skin
Causes whimpering moans.
Icy sharp like untold sin
Stings and numbs to the bone.

Crisp whiteness is tainted
By my sanguine fluids,
Leaving a trail of claret
Traced by wrist leakage.

...drifting further. Coming for me...

Closer they draw,
the hideous beasts,
Teeth and claw
Seeking my meat.

Further cracks and fractures
Capillary across the lake.
My destiny cold casted;
A freezing harsh fate.

I feel water start to seep
Through cracks against my body.
I relax to frozen defeat
And implore god to take me.

...ready to go...

Cracks turn to shatter
And I splash in to water.
Teeth and bones chatter
Convulsion takes over.

The blood from my wrists
Mixes with the briny.
It dances and twists,
A last tragic ballet.

My face finds surface
For the briefest of time,
Allowing grams of breath
To stall my demise.

...I'm fighting...

A bright thought passes
My sad desperate mind.
The vaguest of feelings
I want to survive.

Instinctively I'm flapping
In throes of survival.
And that's when it happened
The heroic arrival!

...I'm lifted...

I'm hurled from the wetness
Of the sub-zero lake
By a mystery witness
To my drowning fate.

Dazed and confused
Half-Frozen and numb,
I relearn to breathe
Through depleted lungs.

...breath; sweet breath...

Through the shock and haze
I absorb a calming scene,
The moon softens it's gaze
And there's quiet in the trees.

The Demons have scattered
In the presence of my champion.
The ice is unshattered.
The birds no longer hellion.

My redeemer attends
To my seeping wrists,
Wrapping them tenderly,
Turning pain to relief.

...the flow slows...

They swaddle me up
In a thick fur hide,
And I lay in their clutch
For a long or short time.

Then from the darkness
Emerges a great steed,
Coat white as virtue,
Eyes bright azure beams.

An old white battered carriage
Trailing in its wake,
From which emerge two clerics
Who rush to my aid.

They lift me upright,
And drag me to the coach,
Haul me inside it,
And ready us to go.

Then we depart
At a breakneck pace.
The coach almost flies
Over frozen lake.

The great white stallion
Whinnies as we ride
And blue lights glimmer
From its sapphire eyes.

...blue lights...
...sirens...

We gallop fast and free
To the edge of the lake,
Then continue through trees
at this blistering pace.

But, as we hurry along
I feel energy depleting.
I try to stay strong
But my will is retreating.

...feeling so weak again...

The beasts from before
Return from all sides,
And chase down the horse
So, faster we ride.

The moon returns rouge
It's face back to gloom.
The birds start to swoop
Sensing my doom.

...the throbbing is back...

The earth again throbs
Like a beating drum,
Jangling my nerves
Pounding my skull.

Beasts come in droves
Wave upon wave.
The birds start to dive
Filled with vile rage.

The evil avian gulls
Snap from the air,
While the demonic ghouls
Lash, gnash and flail.

...a pinch on my arm...
...hot ice in my veins...

The odious ghouls
Relax their pursuit
And the livid gulls
Rise in retreat.

...Energy returning...

The forest undresses
To a vast open clearing,
And shining through mist
Is a huge crooked building.

Great doors swing aside
Light spills out before us
And I'm rushed inside
Carried by my saviours.

I'm whizzed away
Along busy halls
Like a rat in a maze
Lost in the walls.

Oddly dressed folks
Surround my bed.
They prod and poke
At body and head.

My mind is thick milky
Thoughts are a haze;
I'm sure I see witches
Wearing white gowns.

Their hideous faces
Part-concealed by masks,
And Upon their bonces
Sit jagged old hats.

The hands of the shrews
Are frantic and busy.
They attach thick tubes
All over my body.

...voices...
...my name....
...They know my name...

..."27 years old"...
..."lacerations to both forearms"...
..."in and out of consciousness"...
..."administered adrenaline"...

...the throbbing returns...
...I'm drifting away...
...again...

The throbbing drum beat
Returns but much louder.
The room starts to quake,
The lights blink and flicker.

I can hear that sound
From the demonic beasts;
Ached scrapes and moans
As they jitter and sleek.

...unconsciousness is winning...
...I'm blacking out...

The crones at my bed
Chatter and rant,
Place hands on my head
And begin to chant.

I sense the beasts closing
Outside of the room.
The witch hands start glowing
And then a huge BOOM......

...it's dark...
...more than dark...
...everywhere...
...like the bottom of an ocean..
...but there's no water...
...there's no anything...
...just me...
...The sense of me...
...and blackness....
...like I'm becoming the blackness...
...and it's becoming me...
...and...
...a glimmer of light against the dark...
...but it's becoming smaller...
...drifting away from me...
...the light...
...No!..
...it's not moving...
...I'm falling...
...I'm falling..
...away from the light...
...it becomes a pin prick...

...then just a notion of light...
...a fading memory of luminance...

Beasts at the door
Frantically scratching.
The Hags chant more
Their hands now crackling.

"CLEAR"

...existence whooshes around me...
...I'm hurtling towards the light...
...being dragged...
...like a fallen angel...
...tethering back to heaven...
...everything feels on fire...
...not flame-fire...
...like the thought of ancient fire...
...holy fire?..

"CLEAR"

...Washed in cold flame...
...feels like my skin is spinning...
...spinning over my flesh and bones...
...Almost with the light now...
...feel my breath..
...and blood...
...and nerves...

"CLEAR"

...everything is popping and exploding...
...I burst out past the light..
...just briefly...
...a world...
...then it's gone...

The witches are manic
Cackling and shrilling.
A further wild chant
A huge blast of lightning.

"CLEAR"

...I emerge from the dark womb...
...out to a world...
...THE world...
...back...
...to life...
...at least undeath...
...but pain...
I woke up this morn
from a warmer dream;
I'm at the lake shore
And the sun rays beam.

From lost, I was found,
Scared and retreating,
But there's love all around
And my wrists are not bleeding.

Is this me?

I punched the bathroom mirror and shattered the image in to pieces. I could still see myself in the shards at my feet. Little glints of my face; bright blue eyes, peppery beard, the well crafted smile. Well crafted from decades of abuses and undecadent pleasures. Rehearsed, Pre-hearsed and ready for action. The main attraction.

All the sharded reflections resemble me but none are the me I'm searching for. I love what I cannot see in broken mirrors. I want to be what I cannot be in any versions I've measured. I feel like an avatar taking quantum leaps to apparitions of me that I hate and despise. I've existed a hundred times without ever living.

The blood on my knuckles reminds me that I'm supposed to feel. I wipe it around my mouth and cheeks, hoping this will somehow be the key. I wonder if numbness to pain and insanity are the real me.

Or am I just one of the shards the real me isn't searching for?

I collect up all the shards with a dustpan and brush and cast them in to the trash. All that's left is a blank space where my reflection used to be. Remnants of glass dust remain on the floor as tingly little reminders of the shards that weren't me.

Fishing

I'd been fishing for so long; for compliments, for validation, for affirmation, for adoration, for connection, for trust. For love. I switched the bait more times than I can calculate: alternating versions across a spectrum of me: everything from stripped back raw truth to exaggerated shiny-happy caricature.

I have pendulumed between self-worth and self-loathing: rotated between wanton and frigid distance. I have captivated and bored myself along the facades of the realities I have presented.

There we're times I wasn't even sure which version of me I was trying to be: My mind lost in a web of fear and falsity. There were days I looked in mirrors at an obscure stranger; a person with the correct skin-suit but an absence behind the eyes.

I often turned to quick fixes of endorphin driven happiness: brief hot flashes of egotistical relief: pride induced mania. After the buzz fell away, I'd come crashing down in an avalanche of depressive angst.

In the aftermath, I'd promise myself, "never again", in the full knowledge the next 'again' was mere moments away in the bi-polar cycle.

I can't quite pinpoint why or how, but I broke awake, and realised I was existing for everyone but myself. The revelation rang loud, and lessons hit hard. The cheapness of my existence glinted like fools gold.

I no longer cast rods or nets for approval; no longer bait hooks for confirmations. I still listen to the oceans but move in my own sea.

Reformation

I thought, at the end, I would bathe in darkness,
But it's light that washes over me,
Drenching me with burnt redemption,
Soaking in to every atom.
Saturating bright silence.
I feel it, the silence;
It is everywhere and nowhere.

Silence.
Then I rise:

as every shape and shade I've ever been, or will ever be;
Every first and last possibility of my being,
Every diverging variation of versions,
Each spec of cosmic dust collected and combined to every other,
In endless inconceivable ways,
Backwards and forwards in infinite time.

I thought, in the beginning, I would bask in light,
But it's darkness that washes over me.
Shrouding me In frozen reformation.

ON LOVE

This section contains my writings which celebrate love in all its forms; from the grandiose intensity of romantic love to small gestures of generosity with a stranger, love expresses itself to us, and through us, in many powerful ways.

I do believe that embracing love of each other and ourselves is our best path to changing the world, or at least making it bearable. An absent of love is probably the most painful feeling a human can go through. I guess this collection is as much a protest against the absence of love as it is a celebration of love.

"Find what you love and let it kill you"
-Charles Bukowski

We Are One

We are but a drop of water,
Yet, together we are the whole ocean.

We are the tides and waves
shaping and carving the land.

We are each a grain of celestial sand
Which unite to compose beaches

We are the white noises
That conduct the songs of the cosmos

We are the primal forces
Which, in their forges,
Form and cast the valleys
And great mountains

We are the reverberation
Of everything before us,
And the resonation
Of everything to come.

We are the cosmic dust
Which binds all things;
Living or dead,
Physical or ethereal,
Known or unknown.

We are separated,
Yet we are connected,
By the immutable power
Of the universe.

By love.

Until Now (for my baby boy)

For now you are just a thought
in my unwise mind.
A guess.
A prediction.
An intuition.
An apparition.
An uncertainty.

Soon, you'll be here,
and all the fears,
And dreams,
And tears,
will lie before me,
Testing my heart,
Tethering my soul.
Asking me what I'm made of,
And wondering what you'll make of me.

When I Die

When I die, I want the wind to whisper goodbye in your voice;
That tone like hot syrup dripping across freshly woven silk,
Laced with roses and graceful virtue, tinted with sinful milk.

I want your scent to echo in my final sips of breath
As I inhale your lavender and golden odours one last time,
The saccharine reek of your body spinning in my mind.

I want storm clouds to release a furious chorus of rain
Which pitters and patters the syllables of your name,
Over treetops and rooftops, reverberating in the lasts throbs of my eardrums.

I hope that the final touch on my skin is your soft fingers
Tracing your adoration across my tired ageing face.
I want the last sun rays to burn your image to my retinas
So that my dying light is superimposed with your majesty,
To then slowly fade to black with honorable tragedy.

I wish that the last tear to fall on my face, traces to my blue lips
And settles in my mouth, tasting of your sweet caramel breath.
Oh, should my last heartbeat tick exactly as your eyes guide,
Beckoning me softly to that final resting place in the sky;
Me watching you watching me with angelic hues drift away.

One ultimate time, I want your hands to clutch my soul,
And your fingers to weave it around my dying spine,
Creating a heavenly helix, rising up to my cerebral cortex,
Where my sprit and psyche dance together defenseless,
To the tune of your deliverance, bathed in your brilliance,
Then dissipate away to the stars and heavens above,
Tingling and thrumming with your perfect given love.

This is my dedication to you, me and us; this will be my dying wish.

Lovely Lonely

Her hair is just
As imperfectly wild
As her heart
And her smile
Is no less fake
Than her agony.
She hides book smarts
In the same place
She hides her scars.
Abroad from risk,
Away from scrutiny.

In quiet grace,
She's lovely lonely.

She's blinded
To her beauty
By a bitter past
That's made her
Feel used and ugly.
But there's a brightness
She casts out to me,
Baited by radiance,
Weighted with brilliance.

Without doubt,
She's lovely lonely.

She Ideates ways
to find fresh love
Because, she believes,
She needs completing.
Truth is, by herself,
She's already replete
And shouldn't seek
Shallow validation;
And doesn't need

Any more tragedy.

Reluctantly,
She's lovely lonely

Throwing herself
At wrong ones;
She thinks that's
All she deserves.
She coldly snubs
The mild ones,
Fearing
She'll hurt them.
And herself.
Lusted after
Feels better
Than unrequited.

Redundantly,
She's lovely lonely.

In the silent dark
Of distant nights.
Things she knew by halves
Wrongs she thought were right.
The broken calm,
The started fights,
The cuts and bruises,
The dimmed lights.

Despite all this,
She's lovely lonely.

She feels different
But I see same.
Her eccentricity
Will be her making.
Quirkiness will
set her spirit free.
Sweet, Whimsical

And wonderful.
In only a matter
Of short time
The universe will see,
As I do,

She's lovely lonely.

Shadows

Love me
In the shadows
or
Leave me
In the light.

Sorry, not Sorry

I'm sorry that....I'm not sorry.
There's just so much to process,
Apologies for twisted contexts,
In the hot mess contest
We called love.

I have been sorry
In the less bitter past,
Before happily ever after
Became a complete car crash.
With no seat belts.

I'm not sorry now.
I'm mostly dull and numb;
There's no beat to my drum,
No buzz to my drunk,
Without us.

I want to be sorry
I really do.
I want to be there for you
I really, really do
But I'm not....

.....Sorry.

When..

When all the strings
are pulling in discordant
disordered directions,
And your skin feels like
It doesn't belong
On this earth;

When all the gaps
Between heres and theres
Rage like lost oceans
Of thick sorrow
And traversal
feels futile;

When all the light
Sears and silences
Your suffering mind
And looking up
Feels heavier than
Fools gold;

When all the breaths
Burden your chest
Igniting quiet thoughts
With savage flames
Inhaled in chaos
Exhaled as charred sin;

When all the shadows
Come looming
Like fallen angels
Of gods of old
and your bones fold
with woes;

Know that I love you,
more than these words
more than universal truths:
I was born for you
I would burn for you
I will die by your side
Know that I love you.

Dance with your Love

Some people
Will dance
With your love
But run away
When you ask
Them to lay
With your pain

Matches

Loving you was like clutching a freshly lit match;
Hypnotic, primal and free.
Fascinating my total attention,
As light enchanted and danced
Through flickering flame,
Offering bright heat,
While threatening sharp pain.

In short time the fire runs out of stick
And snaps at my fingers and thumb
With white-hot burning betrayal,
Forcing me to release,
Sending blackened wood tumbling,
Trailing wisps of bitter smoke as it falls.
I watch the final flickering embers fade
as they crash to the floor.

A tiny piece of soft wood remains unburnt;
The part which I held as long as I could,
Before being overwhelmed in hurt.
Perhaps I should have used the match
To spark further flares and flames,
Instead of hypnotically watching
As it's fire burnt out and waned.

I'm left like a candle
In a seldom used drawer;
My light only shining
For special occasions,
Or celebrations.
In times of darkness,
Desperate to be lit.

There's always another match
to take out from the box;
But, none I found,
Burn half as bright, Or fast, as you.

The Lucky Leaves

I clung to our fading love,
Like last green leaves of autumn,
Stubbornly clasped to cooling branches,
Desperate to keep us alive forever.

Dying leaves do not choose to fall.
Or to fade.

Cast out by their master -
purpose served. Time spent.
Starved of nourishment.
Left to shrivel and die.

Sometimes, wind gusts quicken the severance,
divorcing a still bright leaf from a still wanting tree.
Those are the lucky ones; leaves that find early escape.

Not bearing the sufferance of drawn out depletion,
Not witnessing themselves amongst final few slaves,
Not cultishly serving the master till the bitter cold end,
Not spending final moments terrified of their imminent demise,
and that of their monarch.
Not believing they have failed.
Unaware their host had used them all along,
intending to cast them away
to the seasonal death cult cycle.

Leaves taken early are indeed the lucky ones;
emancipated from harsh fate,
Oblivious to the horrors of symbiosis,
Death throes spent free on the breeze,
believing their master an impotent god served with purpose.

My Moon

Unlike Jupiter or Neptune
My world
Needs only one moon
Loyally orbiting
Gently influencing
The tides of love.

Love Sins

Last night I crashed asleep,
Drowning in our grief,
Ignoring my second favourite film,
Drinking my least favourite drink.

I was worn out,
And done in,
By you, us,
And our love sins.

This morning announced itself
Via horny birds calls,
And sparks of light
Winking through
Unclean windows.

I urged myself to rise;
Cast off the quilt,
Uncover my pride
But all I found was guilt,
And disappointment.

So, lying here,
Day wasted till noon,
I fail and fold again,
Mourning on you.

I make a promise,
Designed not to keep,
To make the day after,
The day after tomorrow
Less desperate
Than this.

Lips Stick

Those Lips stick to me
Like honey on hot hair.
Saturatingly satisfying,
But such a messy affair.

The treacle juices
Ooze through my fingers,
Covering my hands,
And dripping to my wrists.

I try to wash you off
With futile showers,
And excessive amounts
Of intoxications.

None of it works;
Each time I return
To the edge of burst,
And back to misery.

It might be easier
If I could feel you
One last precious time;
The warm press on skin
The print-mark of oil,
The smell of red wine,
The race in my heart,
The swing and sway
Of subconscious hips,
Please, even just briefly,
Let a few sweet seconds
Belong to us again.

Your gravestone says you were his,
But you were always yours and mine.
I long, and beg, and plead, and scream
Lip stick to me one more time.

Two Ls

Lust
Kicks open the door.
Love
Keeps you in the room.

Sweeter than me

You do things I take for granted
With a brave warm smile.
You spare the time you can
To be my meanwhile.
Without you in this we,
I can't imagine where we'd be.
Each night and every day,
In big and little special ways
You're sweeter than me.

You're sweeter than me baby,
Sweeter than me.
You're sweeter than honey,
So sweeter than me.

During the darkest times,
I get lost in your bright eyes.
Warming my thick cold.
Lightening my Load.
A sugar coated remedy
For my sickly malady.
I dream to find myself a way
A moment for a chance to say
You're sweeter than me

You're sweeter than me baby,
Sweeter than me.
You're sweeter than honey,
So sweeter than me.

You've forgiven and forgotten
A thousand sins and crimes.
Looking past my rotten,
Accepting my wild mind.
You always see the best in me,
always give a chance to me.
Year on year, day on day,

Tomorrow just like yesterday.
You're sweeter than me.

You're sweeter than me baby,
Sweeter than me.
You're sweeter than honey,
So sweeter than me.
You're sweeter than me baby,
Sweeter than me.
You're sweeter than honey,
So sweeter than me.

Lass Kiss

The memory of our last kiss,
A final moment of sweet bliss,
Still sends tingly reminisce
Helter-skeltering down my spine.

The thought of your final touch,
That pulsating heart racing rush,
Still makes my body crimson blush
But I know you're no longer mine.

The recollection of you're solemn face;
You said goodbye as we embraced,
Steers my mind to a painful place,
Haunts all my space and time.

The remnants of the final words,
An ending which I didn't deserve,
Makes skippy beats bounce and traverse
From heart and through my mind.

Future looms empty and grey
Without you in my scenes.
I ache between night and day
Hanging on to old dreams.

Live You

I don't love you,
I live you.
I don't measure you,
I know every inch,
Height, width
And breadth
Of you.

I don't listen to you.
I know the words
Before they leave
Your precious mouth,
And my reply
Sits resting
On my tongue.

I don't need you;
I can quit you
anytime I like.
Just one more
Fix, though
For the road.
Then I'm gone.

Blood clot

There's a blood clot
At the heart
Of our admiration
Which clogs up
Our potential
Perfection.

The arrhythmia
Which we conceal
Has allowed
Our life-blood
To slowly congeal,
And sadly reveal,
Cardiac emergency.

We must dilute the
Thickening flow
Else,
Inspissation
Will decease
Our adoration;
And end
in coagulation.

Sunrise to Sunset

The sun rose today
With you lying on my chest,
And you're laying here again
As October sun sets.
Two hearts next to each other,
Beat upon beat,
Chest against chest.

Izzy (for my autistic niece)

There is a voice inside of you
Buzzing like ten thousand bees.
It's the quiet deafening where
The wind meets the autumn leaves.

One by one the leaves fall
Undressing cold winter branches.
And in that new and empty space
We spectate your wild graces.

Behind those sweet soft eyes
Frenzied waves crash and scream.
And some times, in certain tides,
burns a fierce summer gleam.

I know the colours blur and wash,
where un-peaceful rivers meet,
To smash at battered beaten rocks
And sing out to the trees.

Sometimes, as I watch you float,
With your calm beloved music,
I witness your dim light catch fire
And crackle like burning tulips.

Within minds milky dizzy haze
An untamed angel sits in sin,
Searching for her place to rise
And dulcify the din.

Wake up

We could kiss and make up,
Or just never break up.
Every morning I want to wake up
With you.

Her Past

Her past
Haunts our future.
She casts
A long shadow
And short temper.
I try to comply
But she remembers,
And I suffer
Another man's consequences.

His image
Disturbs her sleep,
But it's my Face
Scratched and bleeding.
His lies
Make her weep,
But it's my mind
Feeling cheated.
His behaviour
Is my disgrace,
And I bear
Another man's penance.

His mistakes
Curse my intentions.
She only sees
Cruel deceptions.
I take her away
But he shadows.
I dry her tears
He wets her eyes.
Familiar fears
Cause loss of control,
And I receive
Another man's punishment.

I try to talk,
She doesn't listen.
I go for walks,
Alone and listless.
The bed is hers.
The couch is mine.
Bills are paid,
But it's not home.
We get drunk,
A fight begins.
She screams,
I say sorry.
Asks me to leave.
Again I go.

It's almost addiction
The cycle we're in.
It never ends
And never will.
I find no way
To sugar the pills.
I've tried to escape
But there's a spell,
Which holds me here
In her hell.

Bliss

We're taught to swoon the "first kiss"
But I,
In dreamy warm bliss,
Yearn to be your last.

People Say

People say, "butter wouldn't melt in her mouth"
But I know her better;
I've seen her sins and horns,
Borne witness to her claws,
And the lash of her unburdened jaw.

People say, "she's soft and gentle"
But I've known the moments
When a fire has roared,
In the pits if her furnace,
And all hell has seeped through.

People say, "she wouldn't harm a fly."
But I've seen red-raw fury;
A blazing whirl-wind,
Unstoppable, except by being left
To burn its path and peter out.

People say, "she's so reliable"
But they haven't seen her wild and free
Spinning and dancing,
barefoot and barely clothed;
While responsibilities drift away.

People say, "She's a rock"
But I've seen her delicate
Fragile and unfurnished.
In the lowest times,
With broken confidence
And shattered esteem.

People say, "she'll never let you down",
But I've been drowned,
Made to feel a Clown,
And left to crawl the ground,
Back to her.

Fix

Revenge cannot
Fix a
Broken heart
Just as
Teardrops
Cannot quench
A thirst.

They want my Bride

They want my bride
In physical ways.
Ignore her mind
View just her frame.

They see my bride
As only flesh.
Her streamed-lines
And perky breasts.

They watch my bride
When I'm not there.
They dig her vibe
And long blonde hair.

They lust my bride
For one night sex.
Eye her behind
And lengthy legs.

They praise my bride
With compliments,
But carnal designs
Is all they want.

They crave my bride
In starving ways.
They seek, she hides
Predators, prey.

They yearn my bride
Those horny young fools.
The want the wild
But have never felt claws.

They'd kiss my bride
Without the vows.
Ignore she's wise
See only the wow!

They'd hurt my bride
Given half a chance,
Cut down her pride
With salacious advance.

They say my bride
Is too good for me.
They might be right;
She's out of my league!

I'm in love with my bride
For more than just show.
Under shimmer and shine
To the bones below.

Together Apart

I never moved on
But never waited.
Life happened,
While you took your path,
And I took mine.

I never stopped thinking
About your warm breath,
Or the fires
We'd sometimes set,
In our hearts.

I still wonder,
In spare moments,
If we could have
Grown together,
Instead of apart.

Grey

Everything is grey,
And not even shades,
Just – Grey.
One achingly in-between
Soulless, dullness.
Except you:
You are in colour.

Obsidian Eyes

In the perfect picture that is you,
It's always the eyes that fascinate.
Sepia, sapient, salient,
Obsidian ocular organs;
Dark as the sin of ancestors,
Yet, bright as fresh virtue.

Those eyes tell me you've seen and escaped more hardship than most could have endured.
Tints of deprived upbringing flicker through a now wealthier hue, like holes in expensive socks.

The light in them is scarred and feral, but the darkness is rich and smooth: Like the chocolate she now affords over sugar-cane.

They glow with hard earned respect and reverence, but dim on thoughts of esteem.
Loud and vibrant, yet soft and silent.

The shadows in these eyes say she doesn't make friends easily, but when she does, it's all or nothing. Fierce loyalty and ferocious protection, though previously wounded by rejection.

They shout, "I am educated and can speak 4 languages. Please try and patronise me; please talk down to me; please test me."

They yell, "I know things - more things than servitude and sexitude. I don't NEED a man, or a woman. I don't NEED anyone. But I WANT someone. I WANT to be wanted by someone."

But she won't be owned. Unless she chooses to be.

Her stare challenges you to look away, yet begs that you won't: daring you to ogle at the rest of her; her hair, honey dripped brown, draping around a face forged in now foreign lands. Wanting you to look at her body, but judging you if you do.

You ask yourself if she would curse you or kiss you : make you or break you : begin you or end you.

They tell of her love of books, but lack of enough time to read. Dark books, of course, because life is so agonisingly light and boring.

They say she is obsessed with thriller twists and gory horror movies, but it's pink flowers and blue birds on her note pads.

They hold suicide and pain in their darkness and shine it back outwards like a challenge to suitors: "Can you stand, kneel, fall and lie with me? Can you swim my depths and climb my heights?"

As she peers at you, half vacant, half savage, the eyes whisper, "humans drain my energy. Take me away from here to nature. Make love to me in fields and on river banks. Sleep with me under starry skies, and wake with me as the sun rises. Speak to me like I own you, and you own me. Punish me for every sin I've ever wanted to commit; and reward my every virtue. Protect me when I don't request it; dominate me when I need you to. I want to be yours; I want to leave here with you. But you can never ask me to do so".

"I can love you if you let me. Or leave you if you make me."

"I will commit your every sin, or sit silently in with your virtue."

"I can sing a siren song for as long as you'll listen, or I can offer graceful silence between each of your breaths."

Her regal gaze fades as she walks away, but her head lightly bows back to her childhood.

You are my sunshine

You are my sunshine..

The sun doesn't need to be loved to shine its immaculate light across the solar system, bathing all life in its astral energy. It does not know; it cannot even think to know. It will never know its glory.

It will never perceive itself as a god, though it is the closet observable such entity. Its solar rays are unaffected by your belief in their existence and do not require devotions or prayers to invoke their power.

The sun doesn't comprehend the lengths to which life has gone to thrive in its warmth. It holds no thoughts of photosynthesis. As spring flowers come to bloom, the sun remains passive to their majesty.

The sun holds no intention to cause barren deserts, or melt icecaps. It exists and, in doing so, all the great wonders we know are in debt to its humble potency.

The sun is unaware of its gravitas, which choreographs the orbital ebb and flow of the planets and moons as they endlessly waltz around its mass. In turn, the sun and all its dancers orbit The Milky Way at unimaginable speeds. Part players in an eternal cosmic ballet.

To our knowledge, the sun is the most powerful entity in our lives. Yet, in the grand scheme, it is just an average-sized star, orbiting a mediocre galaxy, in the vastness of the universe. Uninspiring and uninteresting by itself, but limitlessly majestic through the power it holds and the life it brings.

Like the sun, you are beautifully unaware of what you mean to me. Shining your healing light across my face, you give life purpose and grow love like daisies with every burning breath.

Please don't take my sunshine away.

Heartbreak Diet

I'm on a heartbreak diet.
I'm cutting down on pain,
Reducing hateful intake,
Low drama and shame.

I'm going all self-healthy,
Limiting all the unkind.
Switching out negativity
For fresh positive vibes.

High fact,
Low trash,
Gossip free,
Me diet.

Fin.

So, it's come to this...
The end of all existence as I know it;
All my thoughts and dreams,
Every laugh and scream,
The ecstasies and agonies,
Pleasures and tragedies
Rainy days and summer breezes.

Arrive to here..
These final seconds of me.
These last beats of my heart.
These terminal breaths.

And what is on my mind
In these departing moments?

You.
The thought and feel of you.

Goodbye my love.

Empty Spaces

There are words, and empty spaces where words should be.

There is love, and empty spaces where love should be.

There is you, and empty space where you should be.

Loving Bones

It's so cool, to be cruel about love.
Bang on trend, to pretend you hate love.
Fashionable to fear, and sneer at love.
Openly flounce and renounce love.
Try to tear it down, wear it as a frown,
Love.

Those of us living love
Sit with sad owlish eyes,
Wondering why you despise
The one thing that binds us,
The one thing that can unite us,
The one freedom still afforded us.

Is it because you think of love
As stolen kisses and quick fucks,
Lifted skirts and ripped off shirts,
Lusty thoughts meaning naught,
Broken hearts and false starts?
Or-
Do you still judge love by the actions
Of that sociopath who scarred you?
Did love hurt so much, and cut so deep,
It's mere mention tingles and creeps
Through your betrayed body?
Does the one who didn't stay,
The one that got away,
Still haunt your loving bones with woe?

Love Thyself

Allow me to pose a question: who do you love?
How many of you thought about yourself when formulating the answer? If your own self did not cross your mind, then we have work to do.

Most people are never educated, or prepared, for the concept of loving themselves. Loving others, or seeking the love of others, is taught and encouraged every day. As is adoration for hollow victories and shiny objects. We are programmed for fondness of possessions, obsessions, fashions, new-trends, old-trends, old sounds, new-waves, latest crazes, blog pages, body images, celebrity marriages, reality cages etc..

..But never ourself.

We are experts at seeking external validations and a stranger's affirmation, but we are amateur at self-appreciation. Encouraged are we towards shallow observations, discouraged from deep considerations. Shallow is sensory but depth requires free thought, which is scorned.

Loving yourself is in chin-ups but not the school syllabus. It's in the pounds and ounces of a set of scales, but not in the beauty of our individuality. In the movies boys meet girls, meet girls, meet boys, but they never love themselves. There are a billion songs about loving or losing another, but so few about adoring yourself.

Hate, now that's a different story. We are very good at that. Why is it we find it so easy to hate, but so hard to love, ourself?

The answer is programming again. All of the above comes with a caveat of self loathing. A self loathing society fuels the grand machine. Filling the discontented voids they indoctrinate within us with unfulfilling, unimportant hits of endorphins.

A self loving society is a capitalists nightmare. Which is why they work so hard to make you feel awful and unworthy. Unworthy of success, unworthy of creativity, unworthy of freedom, unworthy of love.

Loving ourselves is the first step to liberation; one person at a time, one day at a time.

THOUGHTS AND REFLECTIONS

As sentient beings, all of us think – granted, some more than others. Our extremities of intelligence and cognition are what separates humans from the general animal kingdom.

Our evolution has gifted us the power of deep and complicated thoughts and the ability to reflect. Most of us reflect on the life we've lived, decisions we made (good or bad), and the different paths we could have taken. Thoughtfulness and reflection are also about consideration of the world around us here and now, and how we fit in to this apparent circus. Reflection is as much about pondering the present and future as it is about remembering the past.

The following collection of writings were all written in times of thoughtful reflection, and cover a variety of related and unrelated subjects.

Cogito, ergo sum
-René Descartes

Teenage Dreams

When I was a young wet teen,
My old grandad, rest his soul, said to me,
"Poetry is for puffs and perverts!"

So, I didn't write
Because I thought
he was right,
And poems were wrong,
But now I know
It's wrong for me
not to write.

F&ck you grandad
For the teenage dreams.

Words

I'm afraid you've learnt the words
But not what any of them mean.
You've hummed life's sweet verses
But never sailed it's wild seas.

You've skipped and played
In the sunlit fields
But never had to yield
The hay.

Run Sister

Walk sister!
Walk like you've nowhere to go,
But everywhere to be.
Step out sister!
With loud pride and quiet grace,
Saunter and Traipse.
Without fear of disgrace.

March sister!
March through pain and blister.
Stamp and stomp
Your angry tired feet
to a once forgotten,
Since remembered beat.
And never again need
You scare or retreat.

Smile sister!
Smile from cheek to fresh-wet cheek.
Don't just grin and bare it
Suck it up and wear it
Proudly beam
Like a cat that got the cream.
Represent your dreams
And be their nightmare.
And, try as they might
To cut down your delight,
Then stand twice your height
And smile thrice as hard,
Be four times as happy,
It'll drive them near crazy.

Dance sister!
Dance in un-alone solitude.
Sketch your dreams through every room,
Then take it to the street.
There, let your rhythm and soul greet,
And the past and present meet.

Roll and grind.
Swing and glide.
Waltz and shimmy.
In fresh new victory.
Salsa your demands
Tap-dance your story
Quick step your pride.
Foxtrot your glory

Shout sister!
Shout like you've always had a voice.
Wild, wise and free.

Scream sister!
Scream as if nobody ever said you couldn't,
Or told you that you shouldn't.
Goaded that you wouldn't.

Yell sister!
loud and proud,
As if it's always been allowed.
Wail from your top and bottom.
Through virtue and sin.
From the heights and depths of your soul.
Fiery hot and icy cold.
From the wetness of eyes,
To the tips of your toes.
Hurl your words in to the darkness,
Through your un-banished
And unburdened lips.
Dam well let it rip.

Breathe sister!
Breathe as if first freed
from balmy salt water
Gasp and choke if you have to
But breathe.
Inhale and really feel it.
Exhale and release.
Revel in its sweetness,

Bask in its peace.

Run sister!
Run like your life depends on it
Gallop with unfettered freedom
And unbroken bones
Run like life might never begin
Or might never end.

Ghosts

Regrets are the Ghosts
Of bad decisions,
Missed opportunities,
And words you wish
You'd said, or didn't.

They curse your past
And haunt your future,
Throwing shadows
Wherever light
Dares to shine.

In late, low times
Regrets creep,
And doubts sleek,
Jump out and peep,
Terrifying our esteem.

Ghosts do exist
Inside our grief
Of young anarchy,
Unfound destiny,
And lost dreams.

Children's Ears

Fuses lit in children's ears
Explode in adult minds.

This poem was not written by me

This poem is not mine;
It arrived,
Half contrived,
To my tiny mind
And exists despite me.

I can't take adulation.
The words are collaboration.
An inherited collation.
of thoughts, ideas and actions.
Meaningful interactions,
Joyful distractions,
and Courageous reactions
That came from others before me.

These words are not mine;
They arrived,
Half contrived,
To my tiny mind
And exist despite me.

From the past
On the backs
Of the wild and wise,
Chastised and despised.
These words arose,
Were evolved
and grown,
Then Eventually shown
To what you might call
A collective intellectual soul.

This story is not mine;
It arrived,
Half contrived,
To my tiny mind
and exists despite me.

I may have held the pen
But the power was gifted.
The importance lifted,
From lifetimes
of graft and grind,
by those who had to earn it.
Those who chose to learn it.
Ancestors whose lives,
distant from mine,
rang out a chime,
that reverberates through time
to my tiny, tiny mind.

This life is not mine;
I arrived,
Half contrived,
With a tiny mind.
I exist despite me.

Whispering Grass

The whispering grass will tell the trees,
And the trees will tell the birds and bees,
And they will sing it to the breeze,
And the breeze will scream it to the seas,
And the seas will do just as they please,
And the world, the world will know.

Train Tracks

We used to walk home
Along the train tracks.
We were drunk in town,
Sober when we got back.

Seven miles we'd trudge
In all shades of weather,
Over ballast and mud,
Chatting shit together.

Then one game-changing day
My second cousin 'Mad Mark'
Came from Belfast to stay
And he had his own car!

Mark was far from a laugh.
In fact, he was a prick,
But he had that fucking car,
So we put up with his shit.

He'd drive us around town
Music shaking the windows,
Acting like we wore crowns,
Looking like total bellends.

Sometimes, we'd circle the estate
Whistle and cheer at the girls.
Most would give us the middle finger,
But some gave a cheeky twirl.

We'd pull up at the shops
Meet with other cruisers,
For a quick pit stop
And meet with our dealers.

Parked up at the park
We'd get high on bad gear,
Play fight and laugh,
Sing, dance and cheer.

Then, one game-changing day
My angry cousin "mad mark"
Totally failed to give way,
And wrote-off the damn car.

We walked to the funeral
Along the train tracks,
Remembering how Mark
Was our friend but a twat.

Future Self

Your future self
Is looking back
At these moments
As memories.

T-Shirt

This old tee was once brand new
And, believe it or not, quite trendy too.
I'd wear it to clubs and cool barrooms
But now it's just for painting.

It's travelled the world, wide and far,
Soaked up sun and played guitars
Raced along in top down cars
But now it's just for gardening.

I met you wearing shorts and this tee;
For some mad reason you stuck with me.
I wore it again on date number three
And now it's just for decorating.

This old tee may not look the best
It's aged and worn and full of mess
But sometimes, when I feel depressed
I wear it just for sleeping.

Alpha Wolf

They act like wolves,
When In their packs,
But on their own
They're soft and slack.

The false alpha male,
Too proud and loud,
Bares his little teeth
And struts around.

So, he's my target;
He's my enemy.
I'll go In fasted
And come out bloody.

Once he falls,
The others will scatter,
Away to their mommy wolves,
Baby teeth chattering.

This new beta wolf,
Sobbing on the floor
Won't be a trouble wolf,
Anymore.

River to Sea

A brother and sister sat on a worn old rock looking out at the vast grey sea.

The brother, being younger, asked,
"Why can't we swim in the sea?"

The sister replied,
"It's to wild and dangerous for us. We would drown. We're not ready!"

The brother, in youthful anarchy, declared, "I have swam many times and many miles. From village to village. From bank to bank.
I am ready!"

The sister quietly replied
"That was the river, silly. This is the sea."

Virtually Virtuous

How easily we signal virtue whilst casting scrolled judgments of sins. How simple it is to strip out context and circumstance; dehumanise the dilemmas of the downtrodden and desperate.

We take such pains to mould and frame our superiority whilst denying it exists. Seeking to substitute hard compassion with convulsions of soft charity. Extracting faux empathy from memes and whimmed stimulus.

Ladies of negotiable affection: The oldest professional on earth :
"Hookers", and "hoes"
Hired and fired without notice
Unwound then unwanted
Tethered to cold desires
And hot survival

"Sell them what they want to buy". Unless what you're selling isn't palatable to grey suited clients who lick the wounds of the very ones they feign to despise.

We've criminalised the survival strategies of the marginalised. Issued them unaffordable fines. Denied the rules and standards afforded to every other profession. Refused workplace protection.

A hypocritical version of morality, in which abject poverty and ethical depravity are acceptable norms, but monetised sexuality is scorned. Pre-teen children work in sweat shops and mineral mines but it the skin curves at curbs that trigger your moral dirge?

We excuse stalkers, hawkers and gawkers : whilst the walkers get sick on the dirty mess. They're dressed to impress. Stressed to impress. Gambling life or death sex to clear healthcare debts.

These fine women are tired but they don't want out : They want in.

Seeking to preach

Beware of people
seeking to preach
Under the guise
of seeking to learn

She saw him

Half drifting in a post-work evening dream,
Auto-piloting her middle-aged,
Middle-priced, automobile.
Weary hands pawing the wheel.
Engine thrumming Its sick old tune.
The radio low playing rhythm and blues.
She saw him!

He still looked so dirty smart
In expensive casual clothes.
Managing to make it look as though
He was doing the clothes a favour.
His hair was longer than she'd left it,
distinctly wild yet un-neglected.
A vibe, no doubt, further perfected
On the women since.

He still had those work worn arms
Full of un-careful tattoos.
Some old, some new,
All without meaning.
Except the one she drew.
She wondered if that still remained;
If it sometimes put her in his mind,
Or a jealous lover made him remove it.

The hate and anger she'd imagined
Failed to find its surface.
She expected to be furious,
But instead was sickly nervous.
Like waiting for that test result,
Or seeing someone vaguely famous.
She felt tragic.

The next minutes she spent choking
On a drying mouth and wetting eyes.
Each inch of him stirring new-old memories,

Which past from her mind,
Through her tears,
Trickled from her nose,
And got caught in her aching throat.

At least, she thought, he hadn't seen her.
If she caught his glance,
Or he shot that smile,
It would be over for her.
She would fall again.
The traffic lights ignored her desperate pleas;
Refusing to turn green.
Allowing her to slowly die,
Stuck on red - for danger.

Quiet Tyranny

The tragedy is
People prefer
Quiet tyranny
To noisy freedom.

Train of Thought

Thoughts are supposed to have a train,
But mine are held in crystal jars,
Attached to zany bumper-cars.
Which bash and bounce,
As they collide and dance,
Across the flaws and walls
Of my tortured mind.

Occasionally, there's a major crash,
And precious thoughts are sent to smash,
Through the gaps and spaces,
Inside the crevices,
And to the outer edges
Of my consciousness.
Waiting for me to pick up the pieces
With uncareful rhyme
And rhythmic glue.

Scattered Thoughts

Fragments of thoughts grace
My tired fractured psyche.
Some, I can almost taste
As my brain conducts prodigy.

Some words bounce around
Like fleas in glass urns.
Fast fated, destiny bound
To quickly crash and burn.

Others ride the endless train
Of my zany wonky mind,
Searching for a place in vein
To exit from the ride.

Some fester in the dark depths,
Hidden through fear and shame,
Caked in untold sin and mess,
Like moss in deep sea caves.

Akin to whales separated
By the scale of great oceans,
Some words wail and cry out
With deep and primal emotions.

Many words simmer and boil
In the pot of past events,
And, as we add fresh new oil,
They spit out over the edge.

Dark-grey stormy skies
Hold little drops of words,
Which build up inside clouds
Raining down when burst.

Some verse wanders lost
Corridors behind our eyes.
Once per while a door unlocks
And out pours rhythm and rhyme.

Some words are held captive
Incarcerated and shackled,
Waiting to be found and freed
From their dank lonely castles.

As suddenly as a tick of the clock
Words can blink in to existence,
Or as slowly as tide moulds rocks
They seep out from cognisance.

Some thoughts gather and flock
And chorus well told songs,
Others fly their own path
To speak of rights and wrongs.

Have You?

Have you tried rising in love
instead of always falling?
Have you tried mindful hope
Instead of hatefully judging?
Have you tried growing into life
instead of slowly dying?

The beginning of free

Like a bird, in a too familiar cage,
Suddenly offered an open gate,
But remains in cowered retreat.
Conditioned to feel defeat.

The outside world torments and taunts,
With a mockery of sights and sounds,
Sweet smells and tastes of free.
Promises of wild-flying Liberty.

It dreams of swooping high and wide.
But could such unpracticed wings
Dare to take rebellious flight -
Or hold up In the sky at all?

The cage may seem livid and listless
To those looking in from out
But it's reliable and consistent;
Unremarkable but safe.

An incarcerated mind
Prohibits all choice.
So, it sits timid and tame
Waiting for the gate to close,

And be unafraid again.

Luminance

The brightest torches
Doubt their luminance,
Whilst the dimmest candles
Flicker and falter
Without concern.

Starless Skies

Imagine looking up
At a sky full of stars
And one by one the lights go out.
Each extinguished flame a lost destiny;
A lost opportunity.

An unwritten story
Or unsung song.
A spark of imagination,
Or untold realisation.
A moment of inspiration.
An unknown destination.
A lost demonstration
Of a wild new discovery.

Imagine all your words
fallen on deaf ears.
Slapped down,
Drowned,
Jeered.
Spat out through tears.

Imagine a voice with Something to say
but nowhere to say it.
You can want it.
You can pray it.
But not say it;
Keep it inside and never betray it.

Imagine committing a crime
Just by existing.
Not even resisting;
Just by persisting.
Soft-silently living.
Privately dreaming.
Is anyone listening?

Imagine looking up at starless skies.

History Repeats

History repeats on me;
It literally makes me sick.
Every time I take a bite
My mouth's but an oil slick.

The bloodied hands
In cotton fields,
And broken backs
To meet the yields:

The nightmare existence
Of plantation slaves,
It still persists
in modern ways.

The tinted skins
Of sweat shop Labour;
The scarehouse dreams
Of Modern slavery.

If they can sing,
Or they can dance,
We pay them bling
And give them a chance

But most the rest
Are left to drown
In systemic mess
And burial grounds.

Like the Moon

He, like the moon
Owns no glow.
Instead, he steals
The light of others,
And offers it the
World as his own.

This gives his ego
Laser light relief,
But, In the end,
He's cold and alone,
With no light
To call his own.

Hope is a verb

Hope is a verb
So treat it as one.
It can be given
Or taken,
Lost
Or won.

Last man standing

He lay, half plastered In holiday sin,
Ceaseless sun searing his soft Celtic skin.
The songs that seemed so sweet last night
Boomed and bounced from balconies above,
Grating and aggravating his fragile brain.
Muscles and bones guiltily ached.
His tongue was at war with bitter tastes; Like soured milk mixed with petrol.

Last night, and into this morning,
He was proudly last man standing.
His friends missing presumed sleeping.
While, he remained eagerly persistent.
Fuelled by drinking and snorting.
Un-rhythmically dancing,
And tunelessly singing,
To songs he only vaguely recognised.

Now he lay half-baked and half-baking
In an unaccustomed red hot noon.
Amongst the stinging ultra-violet pain
A particular patch bit and stung;
Like a cat had clawed his bum!
Minds milky haze started to give way
To lost, now returning, memories.
Last night had been....legendary?

He recalled the tattoo was a forfeit
For being the first one to vomit,
After necking more shots of tequila
Than he cared to remember.
He'd usually perform much better;
But there has been that dodgy paella!
The thought of it returned uncertainty
To his war-torn belly.

His un-rested legs begged forgiveness
As he stumbled to the hotel toilets,
And slumped there in tragic sadness.
Wretched, unawake, half dying,
From the aftermath of intoxications.
Gurning and occasionally twitching,
In self inflicted zombification,
Wishing he'd got the 2am taxi.

Around the pool, known and unknown faces
We're in various stages of rehabilitation.
Some, like him, lay listless and grim.
Others, were lively and full of vim.
Oh how he envied yet despised them,
Unpunished by the nights activities,
Full of unfair high-energies,
While he felt like death warmed up.

A few of the squad had tried conversing,
Which he'd met with dismissive cursing.
So they left him sweating and burning
With the midday horrors kicking in.
His inexpensive room was beckoning.
His post-ecstatic, pre-traumatic reckoning.
A dire and too familiar consequence;
The rent you paid for over exuberance.

The room was marginally less uncomfortable
But was away from the blazing sun,
And free from irritating joy and fun.
His weary mind pieced together a battle plan;
A modus operandi he'd employed before.
Rotating between un-asleep and un-awake.
Subconsciously counting and dreading
Each passing moment closer to evening.

By seven came the harsh realisation
That soon he'd be forced to surface.
The squad would already be preparing.
One by one cheerfully appearing,

with their clean clothes and fresh faces.
Cleansed and purged of all their disgraces.
Ready, steady for round two, when he too would do it all again.

Soul Tap

Our soul taps a tune through our spine, reverberating capillaries of rhythm through every atom of our being. We mostly miss it through unwanted busyness or wanton ignorance: we deafen our ears and numb our nerves to its presence. We block the beautiful thoughts it hopes to inspire with temporary hits of dopamine and adrenaline and caffeine and every '-ine' our species craves. We suppress the hum vibrating through our bones in favour of the discordant beats of alluring drums. So addicted are we to the dins and distractions of life, we find our own silence uncomfortable and unfriendly.

We black out and light up on repeat, each time slightly dimmer than the last, until emergence from dark to light is naught but a changing of nouns.

We spend so much time looking backwards and sideways that we forgot how to move forwards. So long we hold our breaths that we forget how to truly breathe. So far we drift from the light, we forget what brightness feels like.

But waiting for us, without falter or failure, sits our rhythm: the beat it goes on, willing for us to finally feel it.

Time Thief

I thought the thief was time.
I woke and realised
All the mistakes were mine.

Days are lost to weeks.
Weeks fade to oblique.
Years of feeling weak.

Decades of dreamt desire
Lost upon a burning pyre.
My sorrow set it on fire.

I took my own sweet time.
Allowed us to untwine.
No such thing as rewind.

Blame was regret in disguise;
Though you told many lies,
All the mistakes were mine.

Colourful Lies

Somewhere between
All the colourful lies
Is a comfortable grey truth
And life, as it always has,
Goes on.

Colour Series: Blue

It's a travesty to describe you as just blue.
You are a kaleidoscope of many hues.
A cool spectrum speaking truth,
From calm river flows to shark tooth.

Yes, you are a clear summer scene,
And you are a glint of warm tranquil sea,
But you are also the crashing tsunami,
And the dying lips of an un-fed baby.

You are cooling rain on hot ground
And a waterfalls soothing sound.
Yet, you are storms and monsoons;
The breathless colour of the drowned.

You are the prettiest young eyes,
And the mild winter skies,
But you are the tints of our cries
And the ghosts in our minds.

You come with old, new and borrowed;
A promise of a fresh tomorrow.
Yet you are our grief and sorrow;
The coldness lurking in the shadows.

You are a calming caress,
Or the stillness of our breath,
The bruises on beaten flesh,
Life-giving veins in milky breasts.

You are the Great Lakes and oceans;
The colour of fluidic restoration.
Yet, you are entropic dissipation;
Life's eventual annihilation.

Where angry water meets cold rock
And summer birds flirt and flock.
At the start and end of winters clutch.
The frigid tints within cosmic dust.

We witness life freshly washed anew,
And the magnificent cycle renewed,
Wherever we find your many hues.
Yet close to darkness are you, Blue.

Colour Series: Red

Oh Red, where do I start with you?
A plethora of shades and hues,
Palest pinks to dark maroons,
Sun-risen tints to dusky gloom.

You start and end each precious day
With fresh and fading solar rays,
Yet, you are found in cosmic dismay,
The crimson death as stars fade.

Synonymous with danger and risk,
You're found within an angry mist.
You are Mother Nature's periodic gift,
And sadness leaking from lost wrists.

You are the tones of love and lust,
The colour of our cheeks all blush,
But you are also in decay and rust,
And the first shadows of descending dusk.

You are the colour of sexual attraction
And the slapped cheeks of our passion.
The neon lights of negotiable affection,
And the elicit gifts of solicitation.

You are found inside our hearts desires,
The burning lust of epicurean fires,
But you are also a vengeful pyre,
The scornful flames of lungs respire.

You can drunkenly paint the town
Or draw a smile upon a clown.
You are the stains of wartime ground,
The bloody lips of a soldiers frown.

You are the shades within our lies,
The deceitful lips of a sinful bride,
Bloodshot stains in alcoholic eyes,
The garnet wash of poached tides.

You are the colour of war remembrance,
The flowery notes of reminiscence,
And you are in our tribal resentment,
The flame that burns for wrath and vengeance.

You are the colour of demonic dread,
The angry thoughts within our heads.
You are the wetness on abusive beds,
And lost control on days without meds.

You are tones of rage and retribution
The streets awash with insurrection.
You are untold sins of institution;
The Hopes and dreams of revolution.

Forever Thoughts

At the outer limits of my consciousness...

...my thoughts tremble around the edge of a great ballroom dance floor, afraid to take the first step.

An orchestra plays from sheet music written by my memories, and conducted by my mood.

An audience of stereotypes, prejudices and Indoctrinations sit judgementally: waiting to mock, jeer and tear down any thought brave enough to step forward to dance.

Once in a long while, a thought finds small courage and tentatively shuffles forward.

Sometimes, the music plays interminable off-beat disturbed melodies, and the brave thoughts shuffle awkward and aimless; alone and detached. Absent of any rhythmic connection or purpose they cower back to the side-lines and eventually drift away.

But...

When the music plays just right, those valorous thoughts begin to waltz and glide across the marble floor, hoping to capture the attention of their peers.

Others grow their courage, and start to sway and swing to the beat of the soul music. One by one they join the dance, spinning and twisting around, and within, each other.

The dance floor becomes awash with Kaleidoscopic imaginations, inspirations and realisations. Each song sweeter than the last, each beat further filling the dance floor, until a swirling pool of wonderment twists and spins together in harmony.

My words are the souls of these thoughts, captured forever in poetry and prose. Souls which would otherwise have been left to dance until they, or the music, died.

As others find these soul-words, on the pages of books or the glint of a screen, they are reanimated as fresh thoughts in the ballrooms of newly inspired minds. And so the cycle continues.

In this way we, the writers, may consider ourselves immortal.

ABOUT THE AUTHOR

D.B. Wright's body resides in England, but his heart and soul belong to Ireland. A loving husband and father with a passion for words in all forms. Outside of writing he finds solace and joy in his family and friends, movies, and thoughts of travel.

He is committed advocate and ambassador for mental health, working on a volunteer basis to support people with their battles, having battled his own traumas and demons his whole life.

Follow the author:
IG: @d.b.writes
FB: @dannyboywrites

Printed in Great Britain
by Amazon